THE HALFBREED CHRONICLES
& OTHER POEMS

THE
HALFBREED CHRONICLES
and Other Poems

Wendy Rose

ACKNOWLEDGMENTS

Some of these poems have appeared in the following magazines and
anthologies: FRONTIERS, RIVER STYX, SPAWNING THE MEDICINE
RIVER, THE GREENFIELD REVIEW, MS. MAGAZINE, ALCAEUS RE-
VIEW, AKWEGON, WORDS IN THE BLOOD (New American Library,
1984), THAT'S WHAT SHE SAID (Indiana University Press, 1984), A
GATHERING OF SPIRIT (Sinister Wisdom Books, 1984), SONGS FROM
THIS EARTH ON TURTLE'S BACK (Greenfield Review Press, 1983), TIME
TO GREEZ (Glide Publications, 1975), ALCATRAZ 2 (Alcatraz Editions,
1982), THE CLOUDS THREW THIS LIGHT (Institute of American Indian
Arts, 1983).

DEDICATION

To Those Powerful Trees
Whose Roots Have
Tangled & Twined

and Let There Be A Blessing
On My Enemies

First Edition — November, 1985
Second Printing — September, 1992

ISBN 0-931122-39-2

Artwork by Wendy Rose
Design and production by Jim Dochniak, Red Sky Typesetting

This project was partially supported by grants from the National
Endowment for the Arts, a Federal Agency, and the California Arts
Council, a State Agency.

WEST END PRESS
P.O. Box 27334
Albuquerque, NM 87125

Contents

PART FOUR: THE HALFBREED CHRONICLES

PART ONE: SIPAPU

*Sipapu: Hopi Place of Emergence

Sipapu

Hand by hand
bone by bone
 dancing
 on the ladder
 like mosquitos
climbing foot
by foot
heels hanging
 impressions
 of spruce
 cut
 into flesh
thumbs wrapped
in day light
 we   emerge
 we   emerge
travel
a life
handle
time
 like something
 fragile
we fulfill
what we say
in the songs
 name the land
 of our skin
 map on the backs
 of our hands
bone by bone
one people
bleeding
 on the trail
 our ancestors knew

what we do
at night
in the scent
of cedar
        covered
        with clay
        we   emerge
        we   emerge
over and over
back and forth
around the seasons
        Anasazi throats
        Anasazi feet
        we climb
to the top
of the world
we stop
        we stop
        in the taste
        of day light
a sound of birth
        a whirl of blood
a spin of song.

To the Hopi in Richmond
(Santa Fe Village on San Francisco Bay)

My people in boxcars,
my people, my pain,
united by the window steam
of lamb stew cooking
and the metal of your walls,
your floors,
your cracks and crickets,
tin roof full of holes:
> that rain
> you prayed for
> thousands of years

> comes now
when you live
in a world
of water.

So remember the sun.
Remember
it was not easy,
the gentle sun
of June mornings
remember

as you pray
today
for the rain
on the mesas,
> the moisture
> in your fields.

Heredity

I come by my waters honestly.
On these yellow arms
the waters run,
into creosote hair
the waters
bend.

Sacramento, Mokelumne, San Joaquin,
Bear Creek, Merced, Colorado, San Juan,
Cumberland, Missouri, St. Lawrence, Genessee,
Clyde, Tweed, Thames, Swansea,
Main, Neckar, Lahn, and Rhine,
Shannon, Suir, Loch Linnhe

all the parts
of these moist songs
that follow rain
around the earth

plumbing
that shakes and groans
under pressure
of old bones.

Summer Rain About to Fall

Fresno, July

Oh Water I am listening
touch the palm leaf
the small
brown
stone,
wingtip and tongue
of hummingbird,
frantic fall
of dragonfly.

You roll this way
your gray blanket spread
thunder under your foot
your hands balled up
like building song
and breath itself
begins to echo

Coalinga

rattles
its new ruins
picking them up
like old shells

full of pioneer steam,
of the S.P. and morning crows
dusty from the cottonfields,
touching their feet
to that thirsty place,
that dry earth;

according to the sign
on the spine of the highway
these hills are lost

yet merely recede
in a native stretch
west and west;

irrigation canals
have broken the bones
of foothill and valley,
have tied together
the old woman's wrists.

Do the songs return
in the stretch of your flesh
Grandmother, the step
of your dancing foot?

Lost Hills, California
1983 (just after the Coalinga earthquake)

* S.P.: Southern Pacific Railroad

13

Nuke Devils: The Indian Women Listen

I am your mother
and I tremble
      up from my blankets,
      shake and howl at you
      with hands outstretched
      to shield you or to push you
      walking on the cactus first.
I come to take you
to the only place safe,
the only path
going to old age
      for, pulling at the stakes, I am angry
      at the cross and nails, the hair they harvest
      from my hungry head. And if you are reluctant
I will deny
that you are my daughter,
you who burst into this world
with the song of my belly,
      you who beat your hands about you
      chasing the fire away.
      This is my cry, my vision,
      that you do not see me
      though like fog I rise
      on all sides around you,
      like rain I feed your corn.
I am hungry enough
to eat myself
and you
      for my blood runs from the river mouth,
      from my bony banks flashfloods bubble.

I breathe on you
to freeze you in one place
then catch you
as you melt like grease
and as I tumble and whirl
with arrows in my side,
antelope eyes open
and wind blowing high
in fir and tamarack;
I topple the machinery
that rolls in the buffalo mounds,
break from electric trees their tops,
fall completely and forever
into star sand.

Loo-Wit

The way they do
this old woman
no longer cares
what others think
but spits her black tobacco
any which way
stretching full length
from her bumpy bed.
Finally up
she sprinkles ashes
on the snow,
cold buttes
promise nothing
but the walk
of winter.
Centuries of cedar
have bound her
to earth,
huckleberry ropes
lay prickly
on her neck.
Around her
machinery growls,
snarls and ploughs
great patches
of her skin.
She crouches
in the north,
her trembling
the source
of dawn.
Light appears
with the shudder
of her slopes,
the movement
of her arm.

Blackberries unravel,
stones dislodge;
it's not as if
they weren't warned.

She was sleeping
but she heard the boot scrape,
the creaking floor,
felt the pull of the blanket
from her thin shoulder.
With one free hand
she finds her weapons
and raises them high;
clearing the twigs from her throat
she sings, she sings,
shaking the sky
like a blanket about her
Loo-wit sings and sings and sings!

*"Loo-wit" is the name by which the Cowlitz People know Mt.
St. Helens — "lady of fire".

Throat Song: The Whirling Earth

"Eskimo throat singers imitate the sounds the women hear . . .
listening to the sound of wind going through the cracks of an igloo
. . . the sound of the sea shore, a river of geese, the sound of the
northern lights while the lights are coming closer . . . in the old days
the people used to think the world was flat, but when they learned
the world was turning, they made a throat-singing song about it."
                              —INUKTITUT MAGAZINE, December, 1980

I always knew you were singing!

As my fingers have pulled your clay,
as your mountains have pulled the clay of me,

as my knees have deeply printed your mud,
as your winds have drawn me down and dried
                              the mud of me,

around me always the drone and scrape of stone,
small movements atom by atom I heard like tiny drums,

I heard flutes and reeds that whine in the wind,
the bongo scratch of beetles in redwood bark,

the constant rattle that made of this land
a great gourd!

Oh I always knew you were singing!

What My Father Said

when lightning danced
west of the mesa
was this: that for us
among the asphalt
and black shadowed structures
of the city
there is some question
about living our lives
and not melting back
to remembered stone, to adobe, to grass,
innocent and loud, sweetly singing
in the summer rain
and rolling clouds.

Begin, he said, by giving back;
as you eat, they eat
so never be full.
Don't let it get easy.
Remember them
think of those ones
that were here before,
remember
how they were hungry,
their eyes like empty bowls,
those ribs sticking out,
those tiny hands.

Your grandmother is singing
that as your feet fold
and your apron wrinkles
kneeling by the stove
you may hear your clan
in the sound of stirring,
find magic stored
in the bottom
of the basket.

Remember the spirits
lying in the scrub,
remember the spirits
in the tree tops huddled,
remember to speak,
to smile, to beckon,
     come and eat
     come and eat
     live in my tongue
     and forget
     your hunger.

Corn-Grinding Song

1.
My heart is asleep
in the peace of pollen,
        in a wide purity,
        in the yellow squash.
My hands dream
of gathering honey
        from heavy-breasted women
        going into the mountain
        with Hoonaw dreams.
My hips, butterfly-lifted,
crowd with children,
        dip and flow with the sun,
        roll from the granite like salt.
My lips bleed,
continue to sing,
beat the hand drum quick
        relax and flex within the earth.
        Be a bridge, be a path, be tomorrow.

2.
Sprouts
rise
pollinate
blow away
lodge
on badger
drop
from birds
change
the sky
sing us
to completion
burrow
keep
the seeds
within.

*Hoonaw: Bear (Hopi)

PART TWO: HALIKSA'II!

*Haliksa'ii!: Listen! (Hopi)

Drum Song

Listen. Turtle
      your flat round feet
      of four claws each
      go slow, go steady,
      from rock to water
      to land to rock to
water.

Listen. Woodpecker
      you lift your red head
      on wind, perch
      on vertical earth
      of tree bark and
branch.

Listen. Snowhare
      your belly drags,
      your whiskers dance
      bush to burrow
      your eyes turn up
      to where owls
hunt.

Listen. Women
      your tongues melt,
      your seeds are planted
      mesa to mesa a shake
      of gourds,
      a line of mountains
      with blankets
      on their
hips.

Story Keeper

The stories
would be braided in my hair
between the plastic comb
and blue wing tips
but as the rattles would spit,
the drums begin,
along would come someone
to stifle and stop
the sound
and the story keeper
I would have been
must melt
into the cave
of things discarded

and this is a wound
to be healed
in the spin of winter
or the spiral
of beginning.
This is the task —
to find the stories now
and to heave at the rocks,
dig at the moss
with my fingernails,
let moisture seep
along my skin
and fall within
soft and dark
to the .blood

and I promise
to find them
even after so long
that underground
they have turned albino

to listen, to shine,
to wait with tongues shriveled
into blackberries;
and fearful of their names
they will crystallize,
burrow, become fossils
with the feathers on their backs
frozen hard like beetle shells.

But spring is floating
to the canyon,
needles burst yellow
from the sugar pine;
the stories
have built
a new house.
Oh they make us dance
the old animal dances
that go a winding way
back and back
to the red clouds
of our first
Hopi morning.

Where I saw them last
they are still —
antelope and bear
dancing in the dust,
prairie dog and lizard
whirling just whirling,
pinyon and willow
bending, twisting,
we women
rooting into earth,
our feet becoming water
and our hair pushing up
like tumbleweeds

and the spirits
should have noticed
how our thoughts wandered
those first days,
how we closed our eyes against them
and forgot all the signs;
the spirits were never
smart about this
but trusted us
to remember it right
and we were distracted,
we were
so new.

I feel the stories
rattle under my hand
like sun-dried greasy
gambling bones.

Wounded Knee: 1890-1973

1.
I fear to see
where your body burns
leaving red
snakes of smoke — *in ceremony: crossing over into other world*
over the hills
like rainbows
arched between the ages *2 unify 2 events*
back to back —
past and prophecy
assume nothing
but harmony
in the gut —
startled to find
a bullet.

Will they let your hair dry *← questions the dead*
till its clay caves and obsidian shadows
pin you silent to the ground?
Will they crack your longbones
and scatter fragments marrow-sucked
to untrustworthy futures?
Will your fingers bleed
on the rotating blade
that scratches LIBERTY
onto your Indian-head?

Jeanette, Jancita, Yellow Thunder, Anna Mae *historical figures*
Jeanette, Jancita, Yellow Thunder, Anna Mae

2.
Oddly fitting
to have been laid
in a white grave
having hung from a cross
the color of Dakota
sky and red clay mixed.
That there should be
no star quilt,
no song, no hungry vision —
naked
so as to be born again
and release the chattering shackles ⌐
like dry corn husks discarded,
smoking and toppling
over and over
in the slippery wind,
hearing them
whisper, open-eyed,
your claim.
Will they know
in their greed
how it was instilled
like red mother's milk
to steam from our heat,
rise up on strong wings,
cry in thunder voice:
Wounded Knee dies dancing
and my hand forever
holds my tongue!

[handwritten annotations: powerful horrific image; addressed men w/ guns; the purpose of writing the poem; me voice; self-awareness (song); now speaks; (dance)]

3.
my song
fire
is water
is water
my eyes
my lips
water
craving air
frost
clouds
breath of Grand
father Grand
mother
within
clouds
clouds
water
let go
the anger
my water eyes
shout
the storm
is red
let it go
you
wounded knee
anger
water
serpents
smoking leaves
skull
of buffalo
banners
of four colors
sweetgrass
steaming
steaming
water

streamofe consciousness

healing

you
wounded knee
cleaning
healing
rejoining
bone
bone
water
my hand
water
my womb
water
your thumbprint
masked/unmasked
gently
water
undeniably
lovingly
on your knee
sweet
water
sweet
grass
(sage) melting *healing*
into sweat
song
water
water
water
water

they shoot
at me
at all
my relations

4.
Amethyst nails (sung) into our flesh;
no pain in old bones — skulls retain
their grins unfettered by flesh or soul.
                    We only knew
                    to wait.

It is our childrens' children
whose voices we hear,
we who thought that with our bodies
died the whole of the Hoop.
Our childrens' children remember
                    to run, to grow strong,
                    to laugh and sing,
                    to pray, to remember
                    to be antelope and hare,
                    big-eyed and wise,
                    cautious and slow.

It is our final knowledge
that they know us
each part a piece of their hearts;
they will see what their fathers, our sons, never saw
frozen as they were into amethyst crystal
                    trapped in the thunder-eggs
                    til the seed dropped
                    to begin itself
                    again.

They find each other though each might be
a distinct field mouse
in the dry tangled grass of Paha Sapa.

    Reborn
    to wear the years
           and sweetgrass
           singing
           and Sun Dance;

    Reborn
    to swim beyond hills
           dressed in spindled sunlight,
           knowing no one but
           the silence
           twisted in;

    Reborn
    to be finished and, finished,
           to rest
           in the shade
           of cooling moon.

Naayawva Taawi

Left in the field
among big-bellied ewes
tightly rusted stuff of borders,
bales of fence wire
sit in the wind
solid
as if on full bellies

and it was not
the garbage you thought
nor discarded nor useless
but look   the small birds
with speckled wings and black heads
have made their nests there
with barley chaff and string,
bits of alfalfa,
singing as sweetly in the wire
as in the willow.

       In the wind
       of sage, sweetgrass,
       you called us
              guteater and squaw
              savage and drunk
      we who finished in the field
      the job you began,
      we who honored your fine foreign steers
      as you did not
      leaving them where they fell
      dead for nothing, to rot

      as you laughed in your sherry
      from porches and doors
      washed white with your joke
      that we seemed so satisfied
      with what you left

and nothing you can do
will stop us
as we re-make
your weapons into charms,
send flying back to you the bullets.

See
we are strong,
we who are so small
we survive unseen;
hear
our beautiful songs
building from the hills
like thunderheads;
watch
the children we weave
from wire bales and string,
from bottles and bullets,
from steer guts and borders —
See, Pahana,
how we nest
in your ruins.

*Naayawva Taawi: Fight Song (Hopi)
*Pahana: Whiteman (Hopi)

("Whiteman" refers to a way of life, a set of institutions, rather than to male
human beings of European ancestry. It is my belief that all of us, including such
men, are victims of the "whiteman".)

Dancing for the Whiteman

"When I would dance for them, they would laugh and throw pennies at my feet. I did my war dances special."
—Paiute man in Yosemite National Park, 1968

Yes we are still doing it   *— still repeating*
for it's such a familiar trail —   *history*
pollen wind swept against old prayers
having become the smell of cedar smoke
receding from the caves on endless beaches,
having become the splash of a camera lens
about our knees.
Oh we are still stepping high,
broadly wobbling with the gleam
of silver conchas, the tender pull
of peyote-rope through our ears   *dance*
and on our quirts,   *images,*
from hip to ankle   *exploitation*
the shake of shawl fringe,
the tangle of tin jingles
on our velvet hips.
Earth muscle hands grip
the old rattle tight
banging seed against seed   *over & over*
to bring thunder storms in a string
following with the wisdom
of shadows.
                    Spin, spin, running in
                    to where the whiteman waits
                    tongue half in, half out
                    for honey or salt to lick
                    from our knuckles, ready
                    to bind us around
                    his slender bush
                    afire with the bones
                    he is still taking!
                                continuism

Through the museums
and in the books
we are dancing,
inside the computers, the t.v.s,
the streetlights of Phoenix,
Santa Fe stucco and plastic vigas,
the bridges and bottles of Gallup,
the water-blur of old treaties.
Watch the pages flip open
in the senseless wind,
rob us word by word by word
of that most ancient copyright
beneath the piss pine's needled branch,
under the lichen-furred boulder,
about the bay-leaved coastal creek,
within the quills of the raven's wing.
And do we lose the way home again?
Lose the movements of the dance —
the door ajar, the sun slipped
over the western brink
by these lives linked
with faceless pennies?

*Conchas: silver buttons
*peyote-rope: rope made of beadwork
*quirts: riding sticks
*jingles: metal beads sewn onto clothing that clink together
*vigas: building timbers along the roof

Backlash

The cage bars are buzzard down
deeply brown
as if intending to be
a deception of skin
angry and firm as I shake them
in my velocity dance.
They do not rattle
but laugh out loud.

My finger bones,
reproduced in your books,
x-rayed into helplessness,
shatter. I am silenced
and ground under
your bulldozing chant.
Things are kept still
as ghosts are polishing the chains.

It's not that your songs
are so much stronger
or your feet more deeply
rooted, but that
there are
so many of you
shouting in a single voice
like a giant child.

PART THREE:
IF I AM TOO BROWN OR TOO WHITE FOR YOU

Memory of Mares

She must have thought she was alone.
The saddle was spotted
with blood   rawhide reins
        slapped on her neck
        squeezing foam sweat
        into stripes.
She must have thought
she was alone,
the way she bent her mouth
        to the bit,
        dust rising like smoke
        from her feet
that as she moved
melted into hooves.
                        Her spine arched
                        into a cup,
                        tan cheeks balanced
                        as she ran
the most dangerous slopes,
Cerrito Creek wider than a woman
or a horse,
        its rocky banks
        its thin ripples
and her running.

Boulders erupted
and acorns rolled;
the sun was only
a round thing
        she balanced
        on her massive hips.
        The blanket raised blisters
stiff with sweat
and now the jerk
of the foal's feet
within that dappled skin
        denying the sixteen hands high of her
        as well as the rain
running beneath.

The Poet Haunted

Ghosts are attacking me
crowding up from the years
like coyotes or priests,
rosaries rattling
between claws and teeth.

In this woman
of a desert,
in these yellow dunes,
the quiet bunch grass,
there is no galaxy
but pain
eternally recalled.
Ghosts these fathers
Ghosts these children
Ghosts these clans
Ghosts these pictures
Ghosts these dancers
Ghosts these gods
Ghosts these afternoons
Ghosts these pills
Ghosts these kittens
Ghosts these fires
Ghosts these hospitals
Ghosts these bullets
Ghosts these horses
        captured bits of thunder
        pushing in from the Pacific
Ghost winds
        sliding the warmth away,
        hiding the red unicorn fooled
        by an ancient virgin
Ghost of myself fooled

Ghosts these virgins
Ghosts these brothers
Ghosts these Chippewas
Ghosts these mountains
Ghosts these buffalo
Ghosts these feminists
Ghosts these lovers
Ghosts these starfish
Ghosts these stars
        understand now
        how ghosts are made
Ghosts these thirty years
        I sleep,
        they stride by
Ghosts these walkers
        I am left
        to bandage the marks
        made by their incessant
        mouths
Ghosts among ghosts
Ghosts left alive
Ghosts dying
        in my bed
        my body
        my massacre.

The Building of the Trophy

Well, you caught me unprepared
beached like driftwood
on some city street
pink against brown
in the late evening sun
bleached ivory
after all the bluster
of your storm.

I am counting
all my fingers and toes,
taking stock
of what you took.
      Can it be pushed back
      together with glue,
      tied up with a thread
leaving only the memory
of thin seams, a scar
where your kiss
was blown away?

I turn each bone
carefully this way
and this way,
measure the hope or the lie
all the gods gave us
that pain is a vitamin
to make us grow.

I am sure you had it
precisely figured
these latest of nights
in your ghost books.
You must have surveyed
everything, compiled long lists,
nightmares of ritual
each one a history
or a trophy or both.

But even the strongest crows
can't fly so far west
and anyway, Crow,
you are just a bird.

Join the ranks
of the formerly employed,
the fathers, the lovers, the friends;
remember with me the egg,
the infant, my preliterate self,
the toddler pushed underwater
by her green-eyed brother.

Now she is six — see her
point off the years
on one hand and a finger
expanding her immensity
against the chair legs,
against spaniel pups
older than the small pile
of her years.

Now she is twelve
bleeding between the legs;
and thirteen
bleeding from everywhere
with blood-caked hair,
welts on her thighs, her feet,
bullet holes beginning
between her eyes.

Sixteen she sleeps
in the sound of sirens,
in jail, at salvation army;
she is hungry enough
to bite the hand that would feed her
or deny her food;
she curls about herself
like a cold serpent.

Eighteen at last
in the arms of a doctor,
waiting for the singe
of shock treatments,
tranquilizers coated
in blue sugar;
she grins. At nineteen
can't remember
she was chained for a time
to the glamor of speed.

Twenty years it took
to ask if it mattered
how dark her skin,
how slanted her eyes,
how hung in beadwork
the lobes of her ears,
how set in silver
the coral of her mouth.

Twenty-one
she surrounds him
on his Honda in the mountains;
through Nevada, Utah, Arizona
and on; country roads, slippery
streets of the cities then
home and gone and home again.

Twenty-five she travels
on hands and knees,
bandages trailing loose
in the sage, her bones
sticking out
from years of famine
and she is leaving him again.

The arctic turned tropic
when at thirty she found
not roses but mangos,
not redwoods but palm trees
and city dances
on uneven pavement;
books and readings and cocktails
corner her at sea
then attack
so gently.

Thirty-four: she counts
the storm-wrack washed up
on her knees and she writes,
writes these words
to test elbow and fingers,
toes and lips, pull
strands of hair silver
against black against gold
from her mouth
where the wind has strung them
like seaweed or just
like the sea.

Halfbreed Cry

My people cry ashes,
bleed fire from their eyes
like amber from polished wood
(the newly carved crucifix,
the twisted torso) as dying,
the tree searches its roots
for water
> and I feel it
> as a separation
> across which I stretch
> to almost touch them
turning
in the small space
of my life so distant oh
so very distant.

As natural as ants in a mound,
as geese in a cloud,
as seeds in a melon
they have each other
and here I come
like I could place
my own two hands
where by father laced up
the stones of his house,
> like I could sit
> at the tip of the mesa
> and greet everyone home
> by their most secret names.

I am over the canyon in one step,
down the highway, smelling the sea
and hearing distant thunder; I am leaving

my uselessness behind
for the people to use as they will
or to sell like a pot to a tourist
who would not know

the difference.

Decide What To Do with Her

she's no good to her people this way:
tie her jaws shut and her teeth
grinding together will not succeed
in her release; stand off a ways
and howl at her the namelessness
she approached us with,
the emptiness she brought,
the weapons she hid
in her clay-colored hands.

She'll twist to get free,
bite the binding around her,
melt the glue with her tongue
til, yellowed aspen leaf
that she is, she'll use her feet
to pry loose from the tree
and let go alone

but nourished by her enemies
she waits, muscles flexing,
feet gripping the rock;
you are warned, my sisters,
she will stay,
for she has survived
even if she
has survived
alone.

Comparison of Hands One Day Late Summer

My hand held
between leaf
and bud
is white clay
unshaped,
the earth
parched,
the empty
ravine;
horizontal cracks
trace
the bone and fat
of me
reluctantly
it doesn't matter
as I dodge
the droughts,
configuration of colors
mixed up and unsettled,
oil upon
the puddle.

Solid on mine
and strong,
your hand
contains
summer thunder,
the moist dark belly
in which
seeds sprout,
the beginning
of laughter,
a little boy's voice,
the promise perhaps
of tomorrow.

The wash deepens
east into night,
sculpted by blood
and tumbling
there comes
end over end
everyone's names.

And myself jealous
of the bones you hold
so well, their proper
shapes, precision
of length;
those old songs
whirling from your throat
easy and hot
for the dancers
and the sweat.
You and your memories
of berries picked ripe,
late summer
days like this
with tongue turning black
and teeth blue,
a loosely-made basket
bouncing from your hip.
Your people stretched you
til one day you woke up
and you just knew
who you were.

I would mention
my memories now
but who would
want to hear
of afternoons alone
and cold nights
on Eagle Hill,
of being a wild horse
among oats, bamboo,
eucalyptus
and sunset-colored women
with braided bridles
in their hands.
Or would you want to know
that I
who sing so much
of kin
grew alone and cold
in places so silent
the dragonflies
thunder.
Would you
want to hear
the sound of being tough,
or the hollow high winds
in my mother's heart.
Would you want to count
the handfuls of pills
or touch the fingers
that tighten on my thigh
even now

for what is a ghost after all
but dry, years or apples,
buckeye or sage, dry
memories, dry berries, dry earth,
dry corn, clocks, eyes,
woman-place, words,
not enough crows
to quarrel for the seeds . . .

If I Am Too Brown or Too White For You

remember I am a garnet woman
whirling into precision
as a crystal arithmetic
or a cluster and so

why the dream
in my mouth,
the flutter of blackbirds
at my wrists?

In the morning
there you are
at the edge of the river
on one knee

and you are selecting me
from among polished stones
more definitely red or white
between which tiny serpents swim

and you see
that my body is blood
frozen into giving birth
over and over, a single motion,

and you touch the matrix
shattered in winter
and begin to piece together
the shape of me

wanting the curl in your palm
to be perfect
and the image less clouded,
less mixed,

but you always see
just in time
working me around
the last hour of the day

there is a small light
in the smoke, a tiny sun
in the blood, so deep
it is there and not there,

so pure
it is singing.

PART FOUR: THE HALFBREED CHRONICLES

Truganinny

"Truganinny, the last of the Tasmanians, had seen the stuffed and mounted body of her husband and it was her dying wish that she be buried in the outback or at sea for she did not wish her body to be subjected to the same indignities. Upon her death she was nevertheless stuffed and mounted and put on display for over eighty years."

—Paul Coe, Australian Aborigine activist, 1972

You will need
to come closer
for little is left
of this tongue
and what I am saying
is important.

I am
the last one.

I whose nipples
wept white mist
and saw so many
dead daughters
their mouths empty and round
their breathing stopped
their eyes gone gray.

Take my hand
black into black
as yellow clay
is a slow melt
to grass gold
of earth

and I am melting
back to the Dream.

Do not leave
for I would speak,
I would sing
another song.

Your song.

They will take me.
Already they come;
even as I breathe
they are waiting for me
to finish my dying.

We old ones
take such
a long time.

Please
take my body
to the source of night,
to the great black desert
where Dreaming was born.
Put me under
the bulk of a mountain
or in the distant sea,
put me where
they will not
find me.

Isamu

"Rocks . . . anywhere in the universe all you find is rocks . . . "
—Isamu Gilmour Noguchi, sculptor/fountain-maker, when asked
why he likes to carve stone

Your American mother
swims in the rocks
          and may not return
          to make you native
nor pluck the stone
flakes from your teeth
          yet she has counted
          each rock four times
and told you "These
are your faces,
          the feet you will know
          when you come home for summer."
Still among her rocks
she gives you granite
          organs to push blood and bile
          between you and your Japanese father
that fading image
who glimmers and vanishes
          and looks at you only
          when no one is looking at him.
Isamu, boy with brown curls,
boy wearing marble chips in his hair,
          boy whose father does not touch him
          and hungrily snatches back his name;
boy left waving his arms
on the outward-bound boat,
          boy who from the intolerant stillness
          of the fishing village
fished for himself a name,
stripped immortality
          from the face of the island
          and into his divided world.

Isamu, your mother loses count
in the strokes of her orbit
            for you launch every day
            your comets behind her.
From moons you have stirred
eruptions of water
            and canyons twice
            circled by tomorrow.
You tell us now you are free
from the bonds of betrayal,
            friend to no one, continual crossing
            back and forth of the sea.

Hanabi-ko (Koko)

"A visitor recently stopped by to see Koko. On greeting the 100-pound gorilla, the visitor pointed to her and then made a small circle with her open hand in the air in front of her own face, signing 'you're pretty.' Koko digested this comment for a moment and then stroked her finger across her nose; her reply meant 'false' or 'fake'."

with her voice
she is grooming me

sounds

like rain
wind   something
I don't remember

touch me here and here
on the underside
of my thigh   the back of my hand
all over the top of my head

little sounds
mouth warm
good
taste of hair flesh salt

mother
            this one went away
            and this one returned

is this my mother
rain wind touch tickle
of sound

The Day They Cleaned Up the Border

"Government soldiers killed my children; I saw it. Then I saw the
head of a baby floating in the water."
—surviving village woman as quoted in the news

How comforting
the clarity
of water,
flute music
in a rush
or startling hush,
crackle of grass
like seeds
in a gourd
and the soothing whisper
of the reeds.
I prayed
the whole night
to be taken
to my past
for the pounding of rifles
comes again and again
morning by morning
til my two babies lay
with names stolen away
in their beds
and in the yard
where they played.
So many gone
and I pray to be taken,
for the lizards to notice
and begin eating
at my feet,
work their way up
til even my heart
is nibbled away.

I have come
so many mornings
to the stream,
so many times prayed
in the glistening mist
and now drink
oceans
to drown myself
from the mountains
of memory.

But look — that little melon rind
or round gourd, brown and white
in the water where I
could pluck it out
and use it dry, slipping
past me in the ripples
and turning
til its tiny mouth
still suckling
points at me.

Robert

"I am death, the destroyer of worlds . . . the physicists have known
sin and this is a knowledge they cannot lose."
                                        —J. Robert Oppenheimer, 1945

the lines of your arteries
begin to glow   making maps
finger follows afraid &
firm   pale like the alamagordo sky
the white lizards in the sand

are you humming or is it
a wayward insect or the tremble
of your deepest bones. los alamos
trinity   alamogordo   (frail robert)
jornada del muerto   you crouch
in the bunker   hands to your eyes
your light gray business suit
loosened tie   speaking to
transparent friends or to no one
in particular

"it's amazing how
the tools, the technology
trap one"

& you are amazed at the welts
so wide on your wrists, those chains
enormous from your belt.
not even your wife was awake
morning pivot of your life
the radio groaned   you twisted
the knob feeling for
an end to feeling   but the voice
said anyway how your kids went screaming
from the crotch of the plane
mouth-first onto play yard & roof top
& garden & temple, onto hair & flesh
onto steel & clay   leaving you
leaving you   leaving you
your own fingerprints   in the ashes
your vomit   your tears

Yuriko

Yuriko was in her mother's womb in Hiroshima when the Americans dropped an atom bomb there in 1945. Her mother died of bone cancer in 1978 and Yuriko herself was born severely retarded — both the direct effects of radiation exposure. As her mother was dying, Yuriko took meticulous care of her and, afterward, refused to visit her grave. A film record exists of Yuriko's first visit to her mother's grave over one year later; her first act was to place her ear against the stone . . . listening.

       Her father has used
       his carpenter's fist
       to surround the slight
       ivory of her hand.
       The grave is at the summit;
       white marble tower
       looking over the village
       beyond the bright bushes,
       the emerald lawn, the koi pond.

Is this the room
my mother is in?
Long box built
of her broken bones,
washed by morning
mist and stars?

Radiation
came like a man
and licked her thighs;
I was a tiny fish
boneless within
and I felt nothing.

       Her miso must not be too hot.
       Her head must be raised just so.
       She likes two pillows to fall between
       while watching t.v.
       and she likes to see papa
       come home from work.

Her face grows formless
as my hands, my lips push
to her nipples, her teeth,
her porcelain bones.

I am the woman of her, papa,
I am the stone of her singing,
I am the sound of crackling flesh,
I was born of your drizzle,
        her fire.

*koi: ornamental carp
*miso: soy broth

Kitty

(That first night I slept next to a Gypsy and she looked at my hands
and said I would survive. I knew then I would live because she had
said so . . . next morning she was cold, dead you know . . .)
—paraphrased from the narrative of Kitty Felix Hart, as she es-
corted her son, a Canadian doctor, around Auschwitz in 1978.
When she was freed from the death camp, she fled to England
and became a medical technician. Parenthetical statements are
paraphrased from her narrative.

I am still preparing
this tomboy hair
split like cake
beribboned
hands jittery
from the razor
and emptied
of girlhood
so fast

> (Mengele stood there. I had to strip
> completely and then I had to run. I had typhus,
> could hardly stand and was out of my head
> but if you couldn't run,
> you would be selected)

I came to know
the bones of my hands
gripping hunger
like a mandolin
and I would someday
paint the scars
red, renew it all
and show my children
the rails we rode
some of us dying
and some of us
praying, falling
from the cattle cars
like straw.

We approached
crowded into a single smell
and on the horizon
as the train began to slow
the flicker and rise
of fire, a glow

      (You got quite accustomed to bodies
      just heaped up. I carried them from
      the infectious hut; that was my job.
      Like this now: just one, two, three
      and throw them down. I had to load
      my friends on. That finished me,
      that really finished me. My mother
      stopped me from going on
      the electric fence . . .)

Don't let the bones
be cast away
but keep them
like heirlooms;
lock them up
and guard them,
your grandfather,
his sons, everyone.
Forget if they grew deformed,
if they came to coat
the blue of test tubes,
if they resided
for a time
in the lab. Remember
machine guns,
wire fences
surrounded by knives,
mines buried beyond
and buried beyond that
where you stand now
in canyons of clay
burned faceless
my naked people.

Ask the plains
of barley stubble,
the mud marked
by Nazi boots,
        the small strong flowers
            she has
            survived

Ask the smoking
Polish sky,
the flat lack
of mountains,
        the fat spotted brown cattle
            she has
            survived

Ask the birches
tingling black
in brittle smoke,
the words wept
in English,
remembered
in Polish,
tears that wipe
the ovens clean
        and run the river to purity
                she has
                survived
                she has
                survived

Julia

(Julia Pastrana was a mid-19th century singer and dancer in the circus who was billed as "The Ugliest Woman in the World," or sometimes, "The Lion Lady". She was a Mexican Indian who had been born with facial deformities and with long hair growing from all over her body, including her face. In an effort to maintain control over her professional life, her manager persuaded her to marry him and she expressed her belief that he was actually in love with her. She bore him a son who lived for only six hours and had inherited his mother's physical appearance. She died three days later. Her husband, unwilling to forfeit his financial investment, had Julia and her infant boy stuffed, mounted and put on display in a case made of wood and glass. As recently as 1975, Julia Pastrana and her little baby were exhibited in Europe and in the United States.)

Tell me it was just a dream,
my husband, a clever trick
made by some tin-faced village god
or ghost coyote, to frighten me
with his claim that our marriage is made
of malice and money.
Oh tell me again
how you admire my hands,
how my jasmine tea is rich and strong,
my singing sweet, my eyes so dark
you would lose yourself swimming
man into fish
as you mapped the pond
you would own.
That was not all.
The room grew cold
as if to joke
with these warm days;
the curtains blew out
and fell back
against the moon-painted sill.

I rose from my bed like a spirit
and, not a spirit at all, floated slowly
to my great glass oval
to see myself reflected
as the burnished bronze woman
skin smooth and tender
I know myself to be
in the dark
above the confusion
of French perfumes
and I was there in the mirror
and I was not.

I had become hard
as the temple stones
of O'tomi, hair grown over my ancient face
like black moss, gray as jungle fog
soaking green the tallest tree tops.
I was frail
as the breaking dry branches
of my winter sand canyons,
standing so still as if
to stand forever.

Oh such a small room!
No bigger than my elbows outstretched
and just as tall as my head.
A small room from which to sing
open the doors
with my cold graceful mouth,
my rigid lips, my silences
dead as yesterday,
cruel as the children
and cold as the coins
that glitter
in your pink fist.

And another magic
in the cold
of that small room:
in my arms
or standing near me
on a tall table
by my right side:
a tiny doll
that looked
like me.

Oh my husband
tell me again
this is only a dream
I wake from warm
and today is still today,
summer sun and quick rain;
tell me, husband, how you love me
for my self one more time.
It scares me so
to be with child,
lioness
with cub.